TO: Laurie

Love Patty ♡

I want to tell you that I believe in you;
I believe in your mind
and all the dreams, intelligence,
and determination within you...
Believe in yourself the way I do,
    and nothing will be beyond your reach.

— Joleen K. Fox

I Believe in You

A Blue Mountain Arts® Collection Full of Encouragement and Inspiration

Edited by Gary Morris

Blue Mountain Press™

Boulder, Colorado

We wish to thank Susan Polis Schutz for permission to reprint the following poems that appear in this publication: "I will support you...." Copyright © 1979 by Continental Publications. And for "I know that lately you have been having problems..." and "I Am Always Here for You." Copyright © 1983, 1986 by Stephen Schutz and Susan Polis Schutz. All rights reserved.

Library of Congress Control Number: 2002104860
ISBN: 0-88396-666-2

ACKNOWLEDGMENTS appear on page 64.

Certain trademarks are used under license.
BLUE MOUNTAIN PRESS is registered in U.S. Patent and Trademark Office.

Printed in the United States of America.
Fourth Printing: 2005

 This book is printed on recycled paper.

This book is printed on fine quality, laid embossed, 80 lb. paper. This paper has been specially produced to be acid free (neutral pH) and contains no groundwood or unbleached pulp. It conforms with the requirements of the American National Standards Institute, Inc., so as to ensure that this book will last and be enjoyed by future generations.

Blue Mountain Arts, Inc.

P.O. Box 4549, Boulder, Colorado 80306

Contents

I Care About You

I may not be the one
with all the answers,
the wisdom, or the power
to make the best decisions in your life.
That power is in your hands,
those decisions are in your heart,
and you're perfectly capable
    of choosing well.
But I <u>am</u> someone who is
    always here to listen
and maybe help
    those answers appear.
I'm here to wait and hope with you,
to keep you company
and let you know how much I care.
I can't do everything I wish,
but caring about you
    is what I do perfectly.
So I will do what I do best —
care deeply and be here
    when you need me.
These are special promises
I can always keep,
    and I always will.

— Barbara J. Hall

I Wish You Could See Yourself Through My Eyes

I see you question if you are enough.
You question your talents.
You question if others will love you
*   just the way you are.*
You question if others will like you.

I see your beauty when you are nearby
*   and when you are far away.*
I look into strangers' eyes and faces,
searching for the safety, peace, warmth,
*   and connectedness that I know*
*   and feel when I'm by your side.*

You question if you have abilities,
while others question
how you could have time for yourself
while being so busy caring for others.
I see you question
if you have what it takes
to travel down the road for yourself
and find your own happiness.

If you would like,
you may borrow my eyes,
 my heart, my soul —
if only for a moment —
 to see what I see,
 to feel what I feel
when I am touched by your
 precious self.

What I see is only a piece
 of all that you are —
and already I see that
 you are so much.

Feel free to borrow my eyes
 for a time
to help when you question yourself
and as you travel down new roads.
One day you will see
with your own eyes
all the beauty and talent that
others — especially me — already see.

 — David M. Austin

When the World Has Got You Down...

*P*ut things in perspective.
Move ahead in a positive way;
    don't allow yourself to become mired
        in a negative view.
See things for what they really are.
Don't let the little things get in the way.
Do what you can, however you can,
    with the resources you have available
        to you.
Don't sell yourself short;
    you have the power within you
        to change what needs changing.
Face the situation with the resolve
    to remedy it; do what you need to do
        to put it behind you.
Move ahead in the direction of happiness;
    go for your dreams
        and reach for your star.

And remember who's in
    the driver's seat: you are.

— Collin McCarty

Remember that You Can Always Count on Me

When life isn't easy and you wonder if anyone understands what you're going through, I want you... to reach out to me. Even if we find ourselves miles apart, don't ever forget that my heart is filled with so many hopes for your happiness.

I want you to feel like you can tell me everything that's on your mind. I want to be able to help you find a million more smiles and make your days more joyful and filled with all the serenity you so dearly deserve.

When you wonder if there is anyone who
cares completely and unconditionally, look
my way. Let down your guard, and know
that it's okay to bare your soul with someone
who knows you as well as I do. When you need
to talk things out, realize that you'll find a very
loving listener... in me.

It doesn't matter what it's for; if it's important
to you, then it's important to me. What matters
most is that you gently remember:
Sometimes two heads (and two hearts) are
better than one, and you can always
count on me to be there for you.

— Marin McKay

I *know that lately you*
have been having problems
and I just want you to know
that you can rely on me
for anything
you might need
But more important
keep in mind at all times
that you are very capable
of dealing with any complications
that life has to offer
So
do whatever you must
feel whatever you must
and keep in mind
that we all
grow wiser and
become more sensitive and
are able to enjoy life more
after we go through
hard times

— Susan Polis Schutz

I Believe in You and Your Success

I believe
That you can accomplish
Wonderful things
Because you, yourself,
Are wonderful.

I believe
That however tough things get,
You'll ultimately win out
Because life isn't about toughness,
It's about care.
And you care.
And I care about you.
So, I know.

I believe
That however long it takes
For you to fulfill your goals,
You will succeed
Because the secret is
That you are already a success.
And you always have been.

.

I believe
That bright moments,
Warm moments,
Are always part of our lives
If we'll only stop, look around,
And celebrate them.

So consider this
A moment of time — stopped —
To make it possible to look around
And celebrate the warmth
And natural brilliance within you...

And to believe!

— G. Saintiny

Keep Believing in Yourself

When you are going through
a difficult time,
you may wonder if you're making
the right choices.
You may wonder about how things
will turn out
if you take a different road.
But I have come to know you,
and I see you for who
you really are.
You are a strong and motivated
individual
who will rise to meet the challenges
that face you
because you are
a loving and warm person
who loves life.
I know you will get through
this difficult time,
and I hope you know
that I will be there for you.

— Beverly A. Chisley

Here Are the Things I Want for You

I want you to always be happy and to be safe and secure. I want you to be well and at peace with yourself. I want you to get from life all that you desire, and more. I want you to feel free to do whatever you want and to let that freedom soar. I want you to know love and be surrounded by it, to bear no pain and feel no hurt. I want you to be the best person you can be. I want you to share the wonderful gift of yourself with others — how very lucky are those who will receive that beauty!

Above all, I want you to know how very much I care... for you.

— Debbie Burton-Peddle

Above All Else...

I'm here for you —
not just for a moment
*   or a day,*
*   but always.*

Anytime your heart needs reassuring,
*   call on me.*
I'll fix it up with smiles and laughter.
I'll bring you comfort to replace each fear,
and I'll hold your hand until each one is
*   gone.*
I'll let you know you're not alone.

I'll do all it takes to show you
*   that I care —*
no matter what time of day it is,
the reason, or the need.
You see, I'm here for you,
and that means anytime at all...

You can always call on me.

*   — Barbara J. Hall*

I want to tell you that I believe in you;
I believe in your mind
and all the dreams, intelligence,
and determination within you.
You can accomplish anything.
You have so much open to you,
so please don't give up on what you want
*   from life*
or from yourself.
Please don't put away the dreams inside you.
You have the power to make them real.
You have the power to make yourself
*   exactly what you want to be.*
Believe in yourself the way I do,
*   and nothing will be beyond your reach.*

— Joleen K. Fox

I'd Love to Do This for You...

I wish I could make sure
   you always had the best —
like laughter, rainbows,
    butterflies, and health.
I wish I could take you anywhere
   you wanted to go
and treat you to waterfalls,
    rivers, forests,
      and mountaintops.
I wish I could make it possible for you
to do anything you ever dreamed of,
    even if just for a day.
I wish I could keep you from
    ever being hurt or sad.
I wish that all your troubles
    and problems would disappear.

I wish that I could package up
all the memories that bring smiles to you
and have them handy for
your immediate enjoyment.
I wish I could guarantee you peace of mind,
contentment, faith, and strength,
as well as the constant ability
to find joy in all the things
that sometimes go unnoticed.
I wish you moments to connect
with other individuals
who are full of smiles and hugs to give away
and stories and laughter to share.
I wish you could always know
how much you are
loved and appreciated.

— Barbara Cage

When You Follow Your Own Heart, the Choices You Make Will Always Be the Right Ones

Remember that no one can ever
make your choices for you.
What you do with your life
    is your own choice.
How you decide to live your life
    and achieve your goals is up to you,
        and no one but you.
Mistakes will be made,
but you can learn from them.
Always remember to live your life
    in a way that's right for you.
Everything you do should make you happy,
and those who may at first disagree
    will, in time,
        be happy for you, too.
Then you will come to see
    that the choices you make are right —
        if you make them for yourself.

— Jodi R. Ernst

Don't Give Up...
Dreams Can Come True

They say dreams can come true
They say you can have it all
I know you've heard that
a thousand times
as you work so hard each day
   just to get by

I know...
how long you have dreamed your dreams
how hard you have worked toward them
how much you've sacrificed
   to keep hope alive
how patient you have been with fate

I know you may feel sometimes
that you are not meant to be
   one of the lucky ones
for whom dreams come true...

But I have seen...
the fire in your eyes
the passion of your spirit
the determination of your will
the calm and confidence in your hand

I want to tell you that I believe in you
I know that your day will come at last

You will open your front door
    one morning
to find that the world has shifted
in the blink of an eye

You will throw back your head
    and laugh up into the sky

And you will become
a voice in the chorus of voices
    exclaiming that...
yes, dreams can come true

— Karen Kittredge

Do Not Regret Your Past; Learn from It

Far away in the distant past
lie the memories of things
   that once were
and how they have affected
   who we are today.
We regret the things we did not do
and wish that we could change
   the things we did wrong.
We should look to the future instead.

We end up wasting our lives
   in remorse
and pass right by all the good things
that are happening in the present.
If we look toward the future,
we are sure to find
at least some happiness that
will make our lives worthwhile.

You can find comfort
in the thoughts and actions
of those around you.
They will help you
get through the rough times
and also rejoice with you
when things are good.

Just look for the brighter days,
and you will get through life.
Many complications may arise
and things might seem wrong,
but stick to your virtues.
Hold your head up high
so the whole world can see
    how special you are...
and you will make it.

— Lauren Hall

You Can Turn Things Around

You are a special person — one who is given a wonderful gift with each new dawn. You have so many moments ahead of you in life: a thousand blessings yet to come, a world of wonder still to experience, a closeness with all creation. And people who care.

You can do whatever you hope to do. It is never too late to reach for the dreams you want to pursue. There is never too little time to strive, too little strength to climb, or too few goals to achieve.

You can turn things around.
When I look at you, I envision
 a dream coming true
  and someone in whom
   I believe.

— Alin Austin

Positive Thinking Will Take You Wherever You Want to Go in Life

There is nothing more powerful in this world than a positive attitude. It will see you through the best and the worst of times, and reassure you when nothing else seems to.

A positive outlook arms you with the confidence you need to reach for your dreams, no matter how high they are.

If you take chances in life, what you're really telling yourself is that you believe in who you are.

Remember to tell yourself that you can do whatever you set your mind to — and you'll see just how far that kind of thinking will get you.

— T. L. Nash

I Wish I Could Explain to You Why Life Is So Unfair at Times

All I can tell you is that
there are good times and bad;
there is love and hate, luck and tragedy.
All of these get in the way of fairness,
which is why we must sometimes accept
the lack of it in our lives.

If you can forgive yourself as well as others
and if you can learn from your mistakes,
problems and heartaches will be stepping-stones
on your path to growing wiser and stronger.

If you can love yourself as well as others,
you will learn acceptance and understanding.

If you believe you are unique and wonderful
(as I know you are),
then you will learn to change what you can,
make a difference when you can,
and accept the things
you can't do anything about.

I know that you'll make the best
of any situation,
taking from it what will be of benefit to you
and discarding the rest.

I also know that you are wise and capable,
loved and appreciated,
and able to overcome anything
that comes your way.

— Barbara Cage

Embrace Your Own Greatness

Live your life through your own eyes
Hold close your grandest vision
*   of yourself*
Do not compromise your greatness
for another's vision
Talk your own language
Express your own soul
You owe nothing to another
*   only to yourself*
Be honest with yourself and your desires
Speak of your highest thoughts
Be all you held in your childhood dreams
No one can take away your power
*   unless you are the one to give it away*
Walk with your head held high
*   so you can see everything clearly*
Decide daily who you wish to be
Create your own moments with wisdom

Carve out your future with clarity
Become your desires
Expand your horizons
Leave yesterdays behind
Run toward tomorrow
Change your mind often
Learn how to flow with the river
Close your eyes and let life take you
Go where your heart leads
Never give up
Don't believe that mistakes
  are destroyers of life
See them as gifts for future success
Dance on rainbows
Meet fairies
Sing with angels
And always give thanks
  for the treasure that is life

— Lynette Ann Lane

I Am Always Here for You

I suspect that
you are thinking about something
that is bothering you
Please share any problems
that you might be having
with someone (it doesn't matter with whom)
because if you just keep these problems
   in your mind
you will not be able to pursue
your thoughts and activities
to your fullest potential
nor will you be able to enjoy
all the great things in life
because problems, whether they are
   large or small
often dominate one's thoughts
You are such a wonderful person
and you should always be happy
and free from nagging worries

I want to remind you that
I am always ready to
listen to you in an understanding way
so if you ever need me
I am always here for you

— Susan Polis Schutz

There's a Light at the End of This Tunnel, and You Will Make It Through

I can't remove the worry from your consciousness. I can't remove the dread of having to face another challenge. I can't carry your burden for you. I can't even help you carry it. But I know you are concerned, as you should be, and I wanted you to know that I'm thinking of you, especially during this time.

I also want you to know that I'm praying for you and sending you good thoughts. I know that you are strong, that you can handle this, and soon you'll be on the other side, and you'll be fine. I know you're doing all that you know to do, and I just wanted you to know that I care about you. There's a light at the end of this tunnel, and you will make it through.

— Donna Fargo

May Hope Always Be Your Comfort and Your Guide

Never give up on yourself
   or anyone else,
for hope is what keeps life
   worth living.
Hope is knowing that there are
   wonderful possibilities and that
   miracles can happen.
Hope is believing that until nothing
   is left, something good exists
   somewhere.
Hope is understanding that change is
   possible and that anything can
   happen.
Hope is being able to imagine that
   something positive can eventually
   come out of heartache and pain
   and that nothing and no one is
   hopeless.
Hope gives each of us the courage to
   face life's challenges, the
   motivation to move forward, and
   the strength to go on.

— Barbara Cage

Never Stop Believing in Rainbows

There is always a part of us that wants
to believe in rainbows. No matter how
difficult our lives become, we aspire
to find that curve in the road that takes
us to a different place. We search for
the mountains that transcend the valleys
in our lives. When clouds obscure our
vision and the journey seems impossible,
the sun shines again in our lives.

I've been where you've been, and I
know the path is not easy. It's riddled
with detours and disappointments.
I came through the rain, and so will
you. You'll stumble and fall, but in the
end you'll find your rainbow — the
one you keep sacred in your heart.

I believe in rainbows... and in you.

— Josie Willis

I Want You to Feel Inspired Today

I want you to feel like
you can climb mountains,
paint extravagant pictures,
or write a best-selling book.
I want you to feel creativity soar
through you, radiate from your mind,
and bring inspiration to your heart.
I want you to feel weightless,
to really lift up and take flight,
and see the world
in its beautiful entirety.
I want you to make magic,
to make masterpieces, and to create
something simply extraordinary.

I want you to feel good about yourself —
confident, self-assured, and limitless —
and believe that nothing, that no one,
stands in your way.
I want you to stop dreaming,
to take hold of those dreams,
bring them to reality,
and show them to the world with pride.
I want you to know
that the world is your palette,
that you can paint shadows in rainbows
and the sky in a vibrant yellow hue...
because you are wondrous and amazing
and capable of anything,
*   and I believe in you today.*

— Vincent Arcoleo

Set Yourself Free

Set yourself free from anything that might hinder you from becoming the person you want to be. Free yourself from the uncertainties about your abilities or the worth of your dreams, from the fears that you may not be able to achieve them or that they won't be what you wanted.

Set yourself free from the past. The good things from yesterday are still yours in memory; the things you want to forget, you will, for tomorrow is only a sunrise away. Free yourself from regret or guilt, and promise to live this day as fully as you can.

Set yourself free from the expectations of others, and never feel guilty or embarrassed if you do not live up to their standards. You are most important to yourself; live by what you feel is best and right for you. Others will come to respect your integrity and honesty.

Set yourself free to simply be yourself, and you will soar higher than you've ever dreamed.

— Edmund O'Neill

Some Dreams
Take a Little Longer
to Come True

Perhaps you've poured
your heart and soul into a project,
but it hasn't flourished as you'd hoped.
It hasn't come alive
the way you know it can.
It hasn't taken on the shape
of true success.

Now... don't give up.
Sometimes one plan
moves slower than another.
Sometimes it creeps and crawls
along its path.
But just remember, so do caterpillars,
and look what they become!

Wait a little longer
and you, too, can see that happy ending
to your dreams.

— Barbara J. Hall

You Are a Champion

*I know that right now is not
an easy time for you.
You have always given so much
of yourself to all of us
who know and love you.
Now, it seems as if the mountain
you are facing is far too big.
But I know someone who can climb mountains
that others might think are impassable —
and that person is YOU.*

*You possess the unique and
wonderful capability
to see a challenge
and believe you can conquer it.
I have seen you do it before,
and I know you will do it this time.*

You are loved. You are important
to so many,
and you are needed by so many for
different reasons.
You have not just existed on this earth;
you have lived.
You have made a difference,
and you will again.

This is not just to affirm
my belief in you.
It is to let you know that I will
be cheering you on.
You are a champion.
You always have been,
and you always will be.
And when you scale this mountain,
I will be there — looking into
the eyes of a champion.
See you at the top!

— Marsha B. Smith

If Ever You Need Me,
I'll Be There...

*If ever you need a helping hand,
   just reach out and touch mine.*

*If ever you're scared or afraid,
   I'll be right by your side.*

*If ever you need words of advice,
   I'll give you the best I have.*

*If ever you're sad and depressed,
   I'll try to brighten your day.*

*If ever you need a shoulder to cry on,
   I have two, waiting here for you.*

*If ever you simply need to talk,
   I promise I'll sit and listen.*

*Whatever the reason,
whatever you're searching for,
whatever you need...*

*I promise
   I'll always be there
      for you.*

— Erin N. Himelrick

Keep Believing in Tomorrow

Sometimes it gets so hard to focus
on what's really important in our lives.
We tend to let the petty, everyday nonsense
blur the view of our tomorrow.

Sometimes our hearts misplace the passion
for our dreams, and doubt seems to take over
all our plans — compromising the future we
long to see. These emotions that confuse us
or set us back are not signs of weakness; they
are signs of our humanity, and accepting their
existence is a strength we all can call upon.

If we allow ourselves to step back, we can take a moment to look at where we were and how far we've come. We're the ones who must choose either to dwell on bitter endings or use the painful knowledge to move on.

I believe that you can do this, and you will persevere past all that once was. Life is a gift, and although you can't return it, you can exchange it for a better one — one that fits you better, makes you feel more secure, and won't just sit up on a shelf.

Keep on believing, keep on fighting, and don't ever forget who you are and what you're working toward.

I have faith in your tomorrow, and I believe in you.

— Michele Lee

I Know This Much About You...

I know that whatever road you choose
you will find it rewarding,
because you always give one hundred percent
to your endeavors.
I also know that whoever
you encounter on that road
will benefit from knowing you,
because of the special and caring person
that you are.
You have wonderful experiences
ahead of you.
Live each day to the fullest,
and never lose appreciation
for your blessings.

— Kelly D. Caron

I'm on Your Side, and I Always Will Be

I just want to give you
a few words of encouragement
to tell you that I believe you are
one of the best people around
and someone who, without a doubt,
deserves to be happy
in your pursuits
and successful in your efforts.
I know that things don't always
    go as planned,
    and plans don't always
        work out as soon as they should.
But — because you are
    the great person that you are —
    I know that your wishes will
    eventually come true for you.

In the meantime...
if you ever need any cheering up
or any words of encouragement,
all you have to do is let me know
        what you need.

Because I'm on your side...
        and I always will be.

— A. Rogers

I will support you
in all that you
do
I will help you
in all that you
need
I will share with you
in all that you
experience
I will encourage you
in all that you
try
I will understand you
in all that is in your
heart
I will love you
in all that you
are

— Susan Polis Schutz

Don't Worry, Everything's Going to Be Okay

I know it hasn't been easy.
But you've done a pretty good job
  of hanging in there
and taking things day by day.

And I want you to remember...
  Things are going to get
    better soon.

And because you are
  the special person you are,
I don't think it's going to take very long.

I want to give you
every bit of encouragement
  I possibly can. Believe in yourself
  because you really are wonderful.

And don't forget that beyond the clouds
that sometimes get in your way,
the sun is shining just for you...
  and everything is going to be okay.

— *Collin McCarty*

Someone Cares for You, and That Someone Is Me!

If you're wondering whether anyone is
thinking about you now, caring about
what you're doing, wishing you the best,
and remembering you in prayer...
If you're feeling alienated from the world,
with no one on your side, and
you're questioning if there's another
human being who would even be
concerned about what's going on in
your life...
Well, wonder no more. Someone is thinking
of you and someone does care about
you, and that someone is me.

If you're wishing you had someone who hopes that
life is being good to you, that you're coping
well with every challenge, and reaching the goals
you want to reach...
If you're hoping that there is someone in your
corner of the world that you could call on any
time, someone with whom you could share
your hopes and dreams and disappointments...
Well, don't waste your time wishing and wondering
anymore. I'd be glad to be that someone. All
you have to do is let me know and I'll be there.

If you need someone to talk to, to share your worries
with, to wish for you perfect health, prosperity,
peace, and happiness...
If you want someone to point out your good qualities
because you just need lifting up, someone to
be on your side no matter what and
to go with you whatever distance you
have to go...
Then look no further than my direction, and don't
give it a second thought. Know that someone is
thinking of you and someone cares about you,
and that someone is me.

— *Donna Fargo*

I Believe in You

*I believe in the way that you are
and the way you will be.
I believe in the things that you say.
You mean the world to me.
And if you should go,
if you should turn around one day,
if you ever should doubt your dreams
in any way,
don't think twice about it.
Don't worry too long
about whether you'll find a place
for yourself in the world — you belong.
I know that you'll get where
you're going someday.
For no matter what happens,
you will find a way.
I believe in the way that you are
and the way you will be.
You are a Shining Star
in this world...*

*and you mean the world
to me.*

— Ashley Rice

ACKNOWLEDGMENTS

The following is a partial list of authors whom the publisher especially wishes to thank for permission to reprint their works.

David M. Austin for "I Wish You Could See Yourself Through My Eyes." Copyright © 2002 by David M. Austin. All rights reserved.

G. Saintiny for "I Believe in You and Your Success." Copyright © 2002 by G. Saintiny. All rights reserved.

Barbara J. Hall for "Above All Else..." and "Some Dreams Take a Little Longer to Come True." Copyright © 2002 by Barbara J. Hall. All rights reserved.

Karen Kittredge for "Don't Give Up... Dreams Can Come True." Copyright © 2002 by Karen Kittredge. All rights reserved.

Lauren Hall for "Do Not Regret Your Past; Learn from It." Copyright © 2002 by Lauren Hall. All rights reserved.

T. L. Nash for "Positive Thinking Will Take You Wherever You Want to Go in Life." Copyright © 2002 by T. L. Nash. All rights reserved.

Lynette Ann Lane for "Embrace Your Own Greatness." Copyright © 2002 by Lynette Ann Lane. All rights reserved.

PrimaDonna Entertainment Corp. for the following by Donna Fargo: "There's a Light at the End of This Tunnel, and You Will Make It Through" and "Someone Cares for You, and That Someone Is Me!" Copyright © 1996, 2002 by PrimaDonna Entertainment Corp. All rights reserved.

Barbara Cage for "May Hope Always Be Your Comfort and Your Guide." Copyright © 2002 by Barbara Cage. All rights reserved.

Josie Willis for "Never Stop Believing in Rainbows." Copyright © 2002 by Josie Willis. All rights reserved.

Marsha B. Smith for "You Are a Champion." Copyright © 2002 by Marsha B. Smith. All rights reserved.

Michele Lee for "Keep Believing in Tomorrow." Copyright © 2002 by Michele Lee. All rights reserved.

A careful effort has been made to trace the ownership of poems used in this anthology in order to obtain permission to reprint copyrighted materials and give proper credit to the copyright owners. If any error or omission has occurred, it is completely inadvertent, and we would like to make corrections in future editions provided that written notification is made to the publisher:

BLUE MOUNTAIN ARTS, INC., P.O. Box 4549, Boulder, Colorado 80306